THIS BOOK

 _____

Date: _____

Departure Location	Departure Time
Stopover	Time
Arrival Location	Date & Time

Weather
Wind
Forecast
Visibility
Wave

Course / Coordinates
Speed
Distance
Crew

Sketch	Notes

Photo

Anecdotes / Special Moments

Route

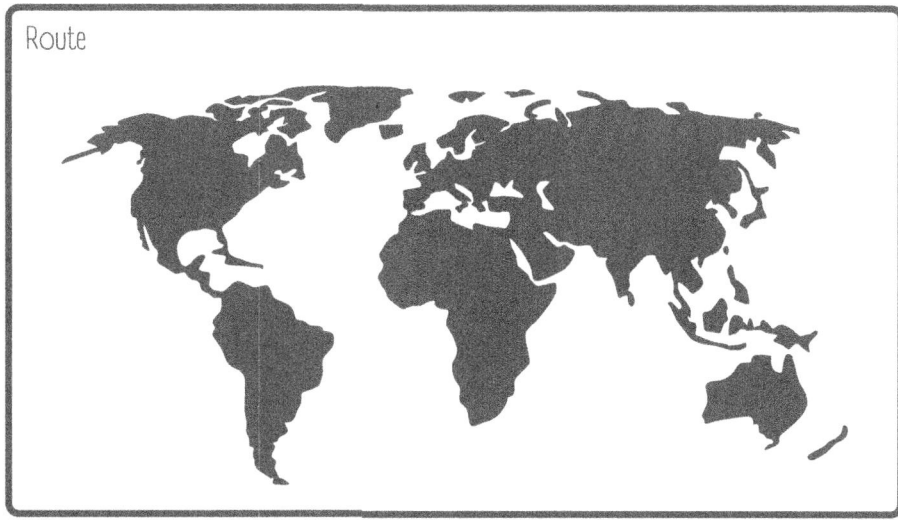

Date: _____

Departure Location	Departure Time
Stopover	Time
Arrival Location	Date & Time

Weather
Wind
Forecast
Visibility
Wave

Course / Coordinates
Speed
Distance
Crew

Sketch	Notes

Photo

Anecdotes / Special Moments

Route

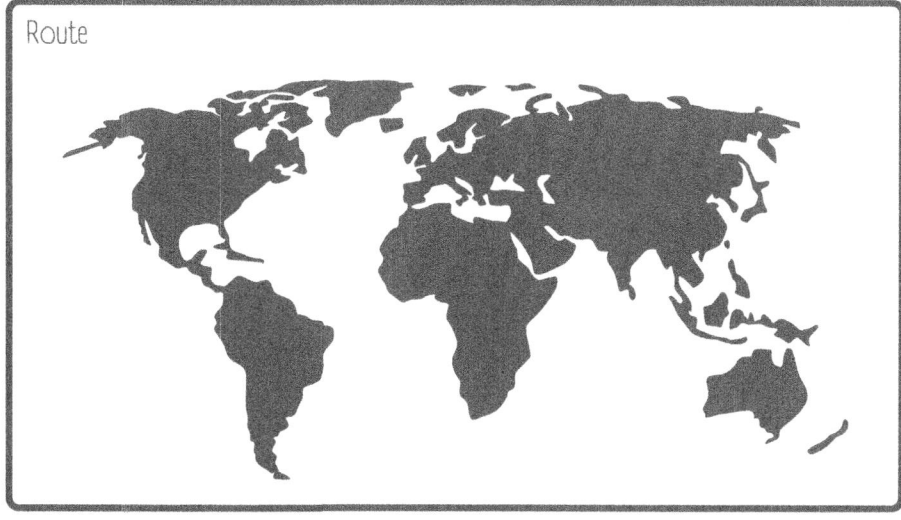

Date: _____

Departure Location	Departure Time
Stopover	Time
Arrival Location	Date & Time

Weather
Wind
Forecast
Visibility
Wave

Course / Coordinates
Speed
Distance
Crew

Sketch	Notes

Photo

Anecdotes / Special Moments

Route

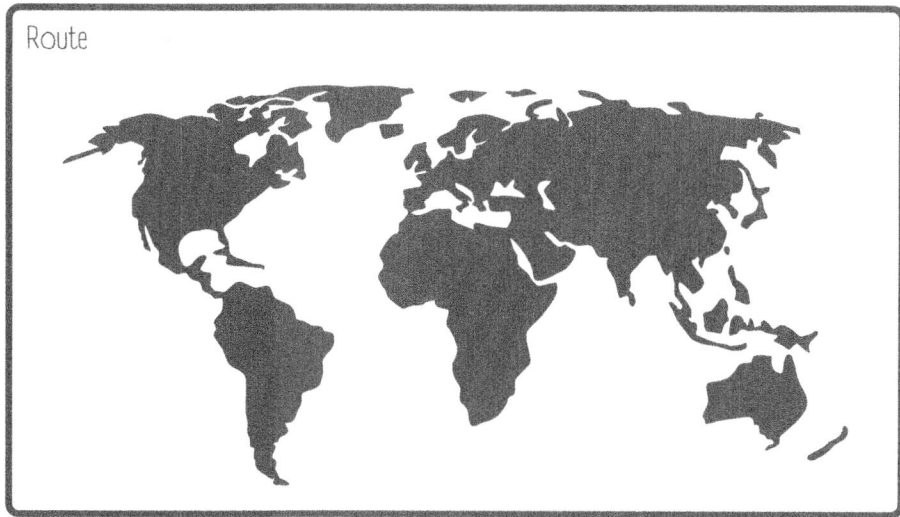

Date: ....

Departure Location	Departure Time
Stopover	Time
Arrival Location	Date & Time

Weather
Wind
Forecast
Visibility
Wave

Course / Coordinates
Speed
Distance
Crew

Sketch	Notes

Photo

Anecdotes / Special Moments

Route

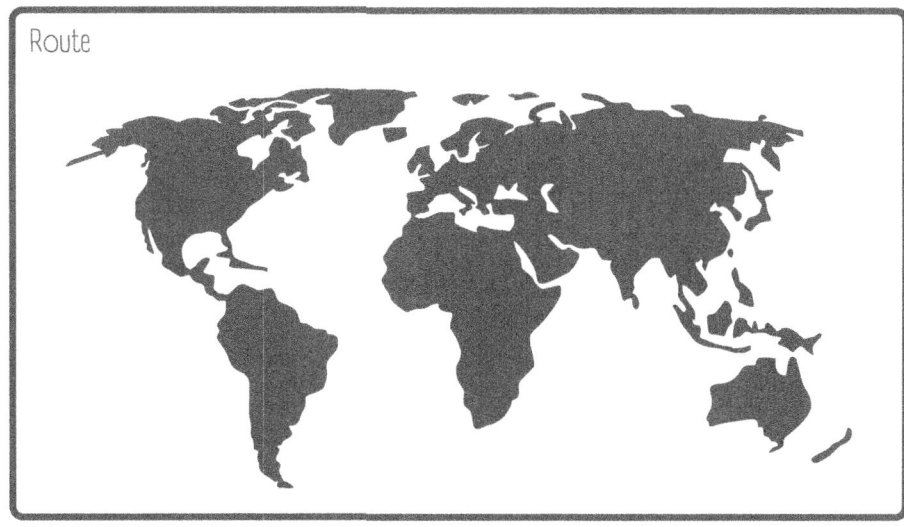

Date: _____

Departure Location	Departure Time
Stopover	Time
Arrival Location	Date & Time

Weather
Wind
Forecast
Visibility
Wave

Course / Coordinates
Speed
Distance
Crew

Sketch	Notes

Photo

Anecdotes / Special Moments

Route

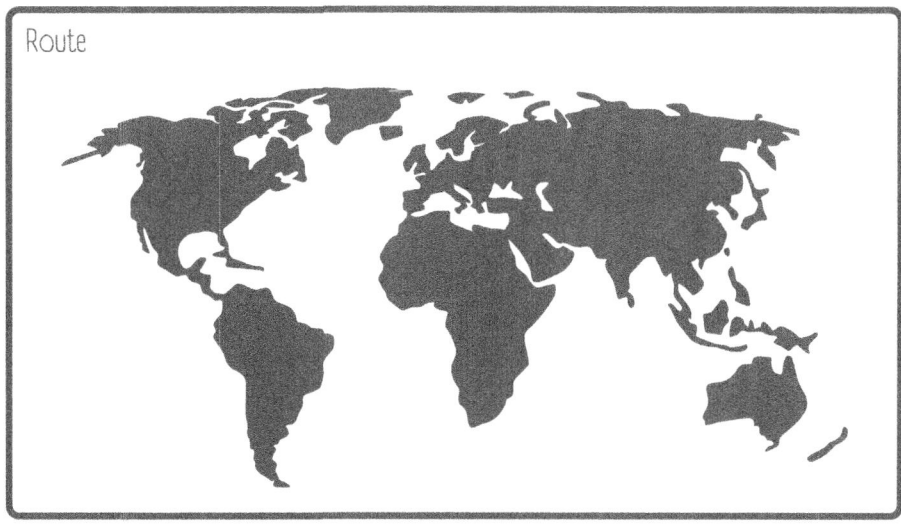

Date: _____

Departure Location	Departure Time
Stopover	Time
Arrival Location	Date & Time

Weather
Wind
Forecast
Visibility
Wave

Course / Coordinates
Speed
Distance
Crew

Sketch	Notes

Photo

Anecdotes / Special Moments

Route

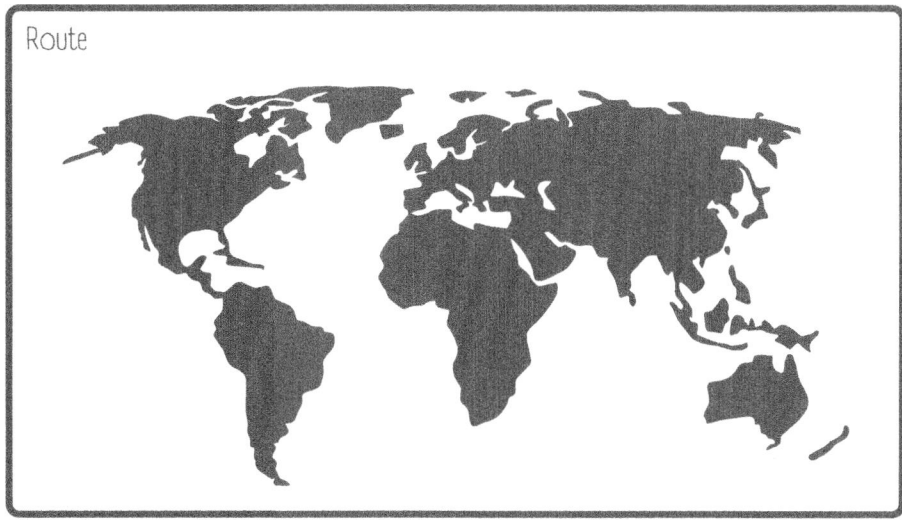

Date: _____

Departure Location	Departure Time
Stopover	Time
Arrival Location	Date & Time

Weather	
Wind	
Forecast	
Visibility	
Wave	

Course / Coordinates	
Speed	
Distance	
Crew	

Sketch	Notes

Photo

Anecdotes / Special Moments

Route

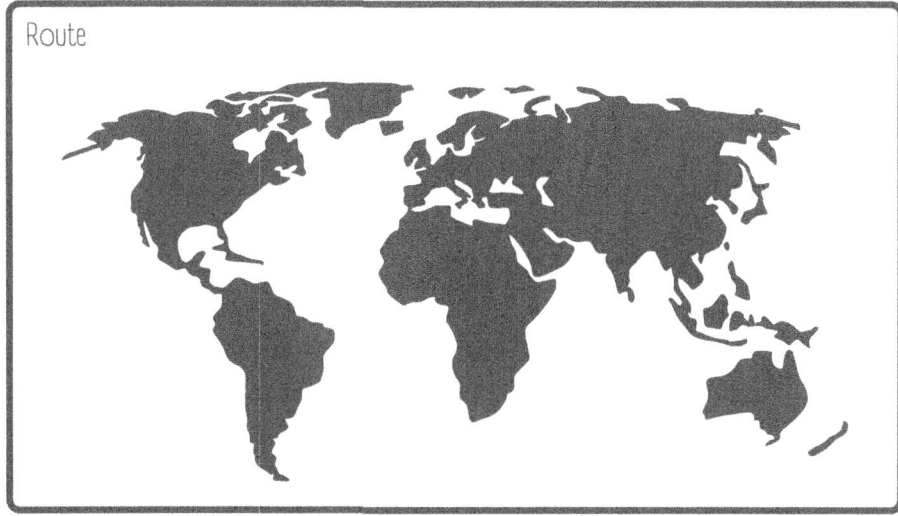

Date: _____

Departure Location	Departure Time
Stopover	Time
Arrival Location	Date & Time

Weather
Wind
Forecast
Visibility
Wave

Course / Coordinates
Speed
Distance
Crew

Sketch	Notes

Photo

Anecdotes / Special Moments

Route

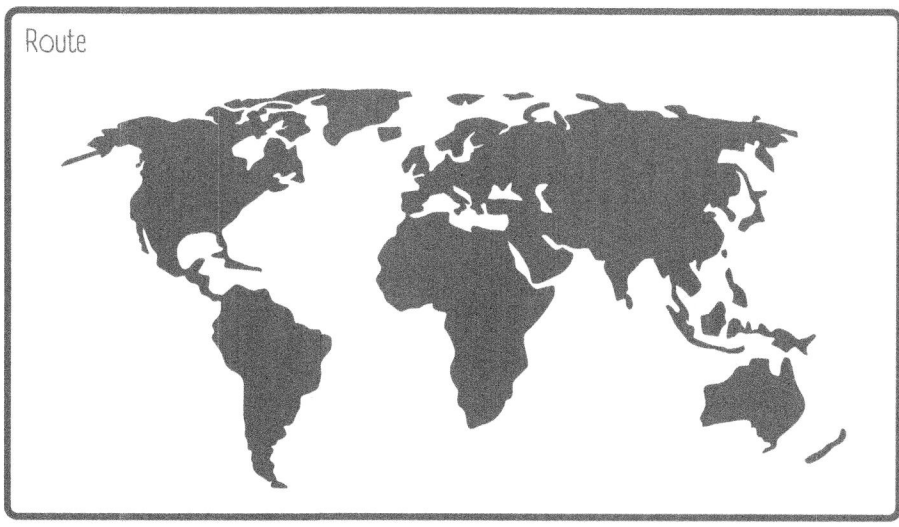

Date: _____

Departure Location	Departure Time
Stopover	Time
Arrival Location	Date & Time

Weather
Wind
Forecast
Visibility
Wave

Course / Coordinates
Speed
Distance
Crew

Sketch	Notes

Photo

Anecdotes / Special Moments

Route

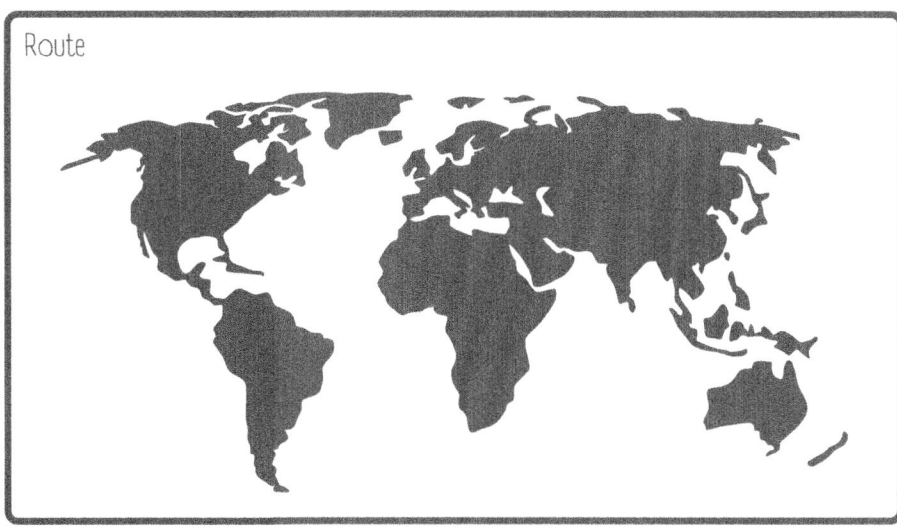

Date: _____

Departure Location	Departure Time
Stopover	Time
Arrival Location	Date & Time

Weather
Wind
Forecast
Visibility
Wave

Course / Coordinates
Speed
Distance
Crew

Sketch	Notes

Photo

Anecdotes / Special Moments

Route

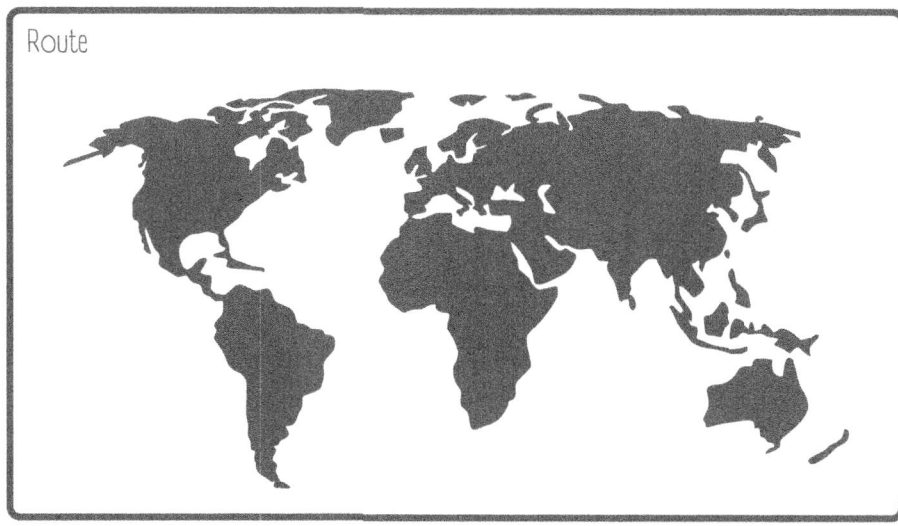

Date: ....

Departure Location	Departure Time
Stopover	Time
Arrival Location	Date & Time

Weather
Wind
Forecast
Visibility
Wave

Course / Coordinates
Speed
Distance
Crew

Sketch	Notes

Photo

Anecdotes / Special Moments

Route

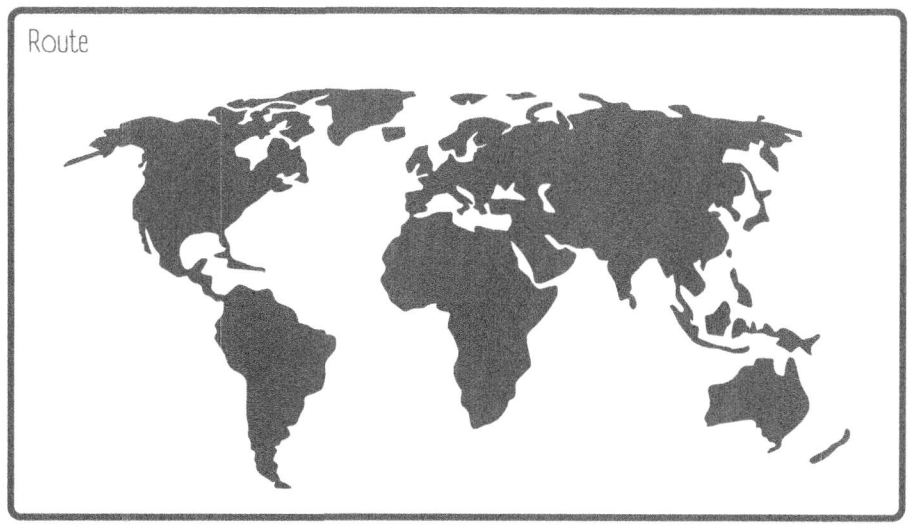

Date: _____

Departure Location	Departure Time
Stopover	Time
Arrival Location	Date & Time

Weather	
Wind	
Forecast	
Visibility	
Wave	

Course / Coordinates	
Speed	
Distance	
Crew	

Sketch	Notes

Photo

Anecdotes / Special Moments

Route

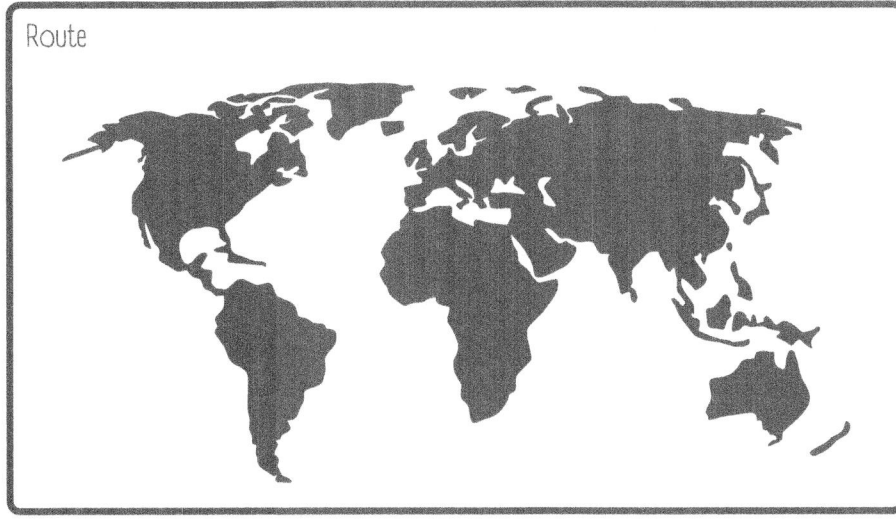

Date: ....

Departure Location	Departure Time
Stopover	Time
Arrival Location	Date & Time

Weather	
Wind	
Forecast	
Visibility	
Wave	

Course / Coordinates	
Speed	
Distance	
Crew	

Sketch	Notes

Photo

Anecdotes / Special Moments

Route

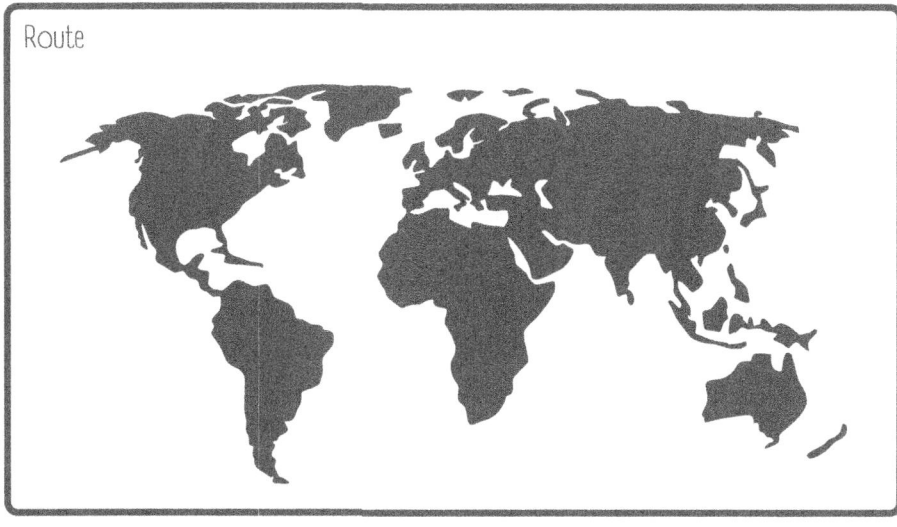

Date: ....

Departure Location	Departure Time
Stopover	Time
Arrival Location	Date & Time

Weather
Wind
Forecast
Visibility
Wave

Course / Coordinates
Speed
Distance
Crew

Sketch	Notes

Photo

Anecdotes / Special Moments

Route

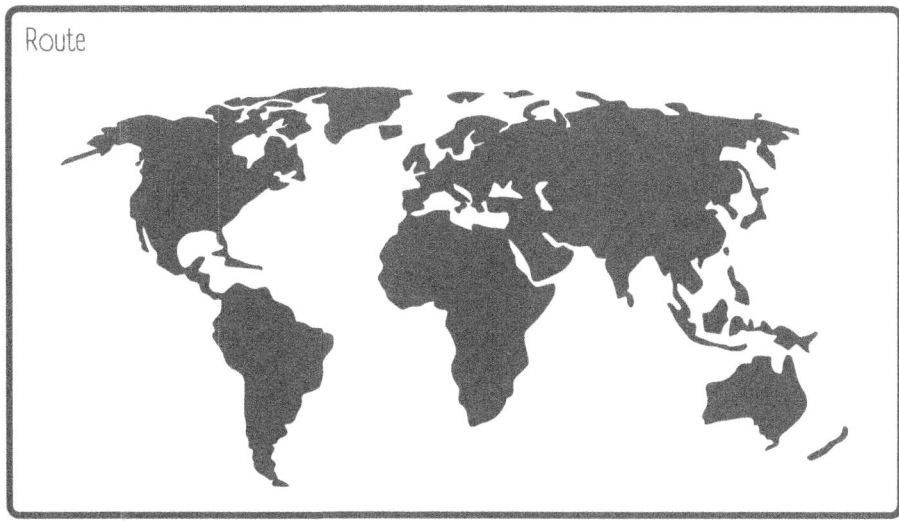

Date: ....

Departure Location	Departure Time
Stopover	Time
Arrival Location	Date & Time

Weather
Wind
Forecast
Visibility
Wave

Course / Coordinates
Speed
Distance
Crew

Sketch	Notes

Photo

Anecdotes / Special Moments

Route

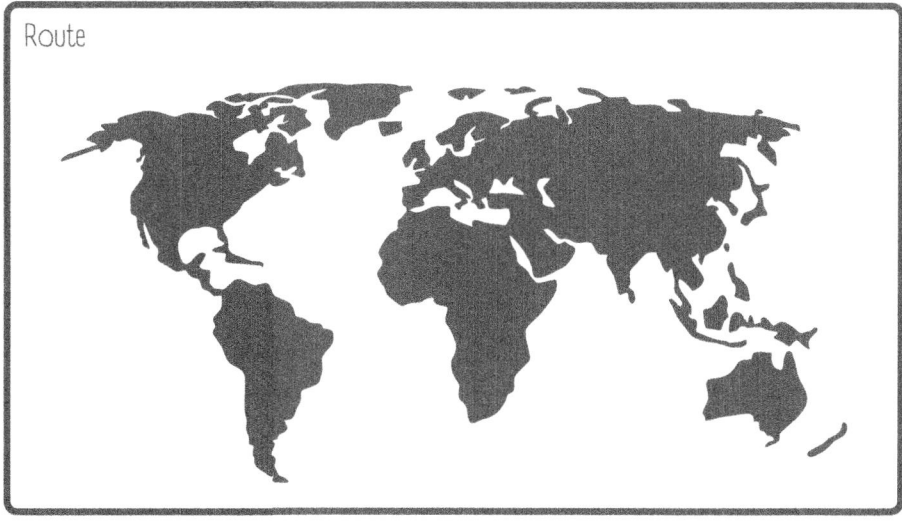

Date: ....

Departure Location	Departure Time
Stopover	Time
Arrival Location	Date & Time

Weather
Wind
Forecast
Visibility
Wave

Course / Coordinates
Speed
Distance
Crew

Sketch	Notes

Photo

Anecdotes / Special Moments

Route

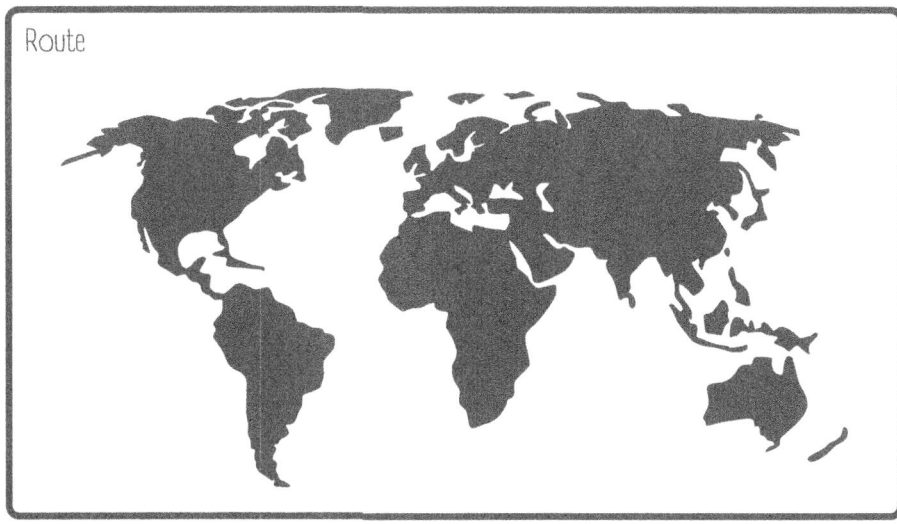

Date: ....

Departure Location	Departure Time
Stopover	Time
Arrival Location	Date & Time

Weather	
Wind	
Forecast	
Visibility	
Wave	

Course / Coordinates	
Speed	
Distance	
Crew	

Sketch	Notes

Photo

Anecdotes / Special Moments

Route

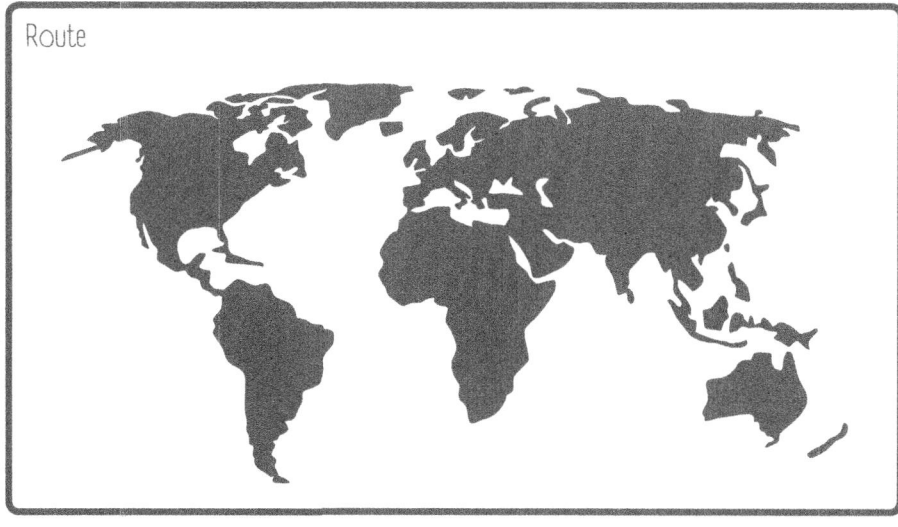

Date:

Departure Location	Departure Time
Stopover	Time
Arrival Location	Date & Time

Weather
Wind
Forecast
Visibility
Wave

Course / Coordinates
Speed
Distance
Crew

Sketch	Notes

Photo

Anecdotes / Special Moments

Route

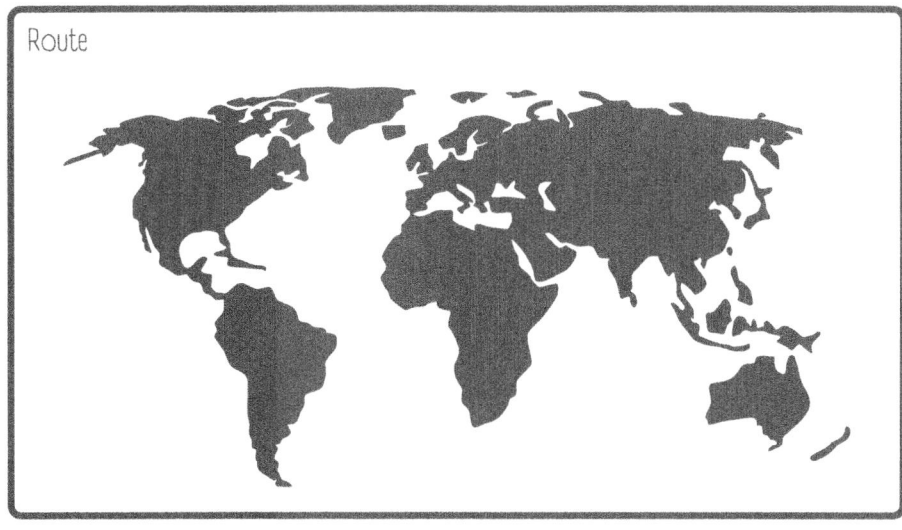

Date: _____

Departure Location	Departure Time
Stopover	Time
Arrival Location	Date & Time

Weather
Wind
Forecast
Visibility
Wave

Course / Coordinates
Speed
Distance
Crew

Sketch	Notes

Photo

Anecdotes / Special Moments

Route

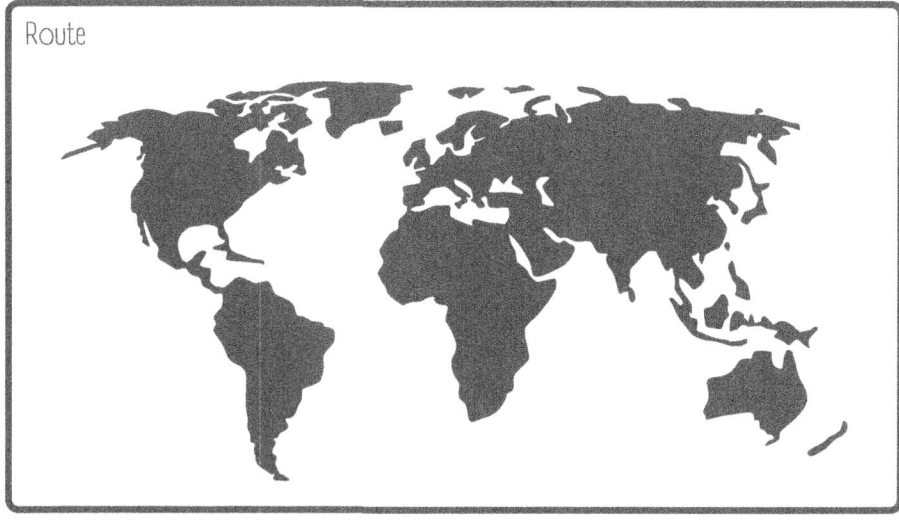

Date: ....

Departure Location	Departure Time
Stopover	Time
Arrival Location	Date & Time

Weather
Wind
Forecast
Visibility
Wave

Course / Coordinates
Speed
Distance
Crew

Sketch	Notes

Photo

Anecdotes / Special Moments

Route

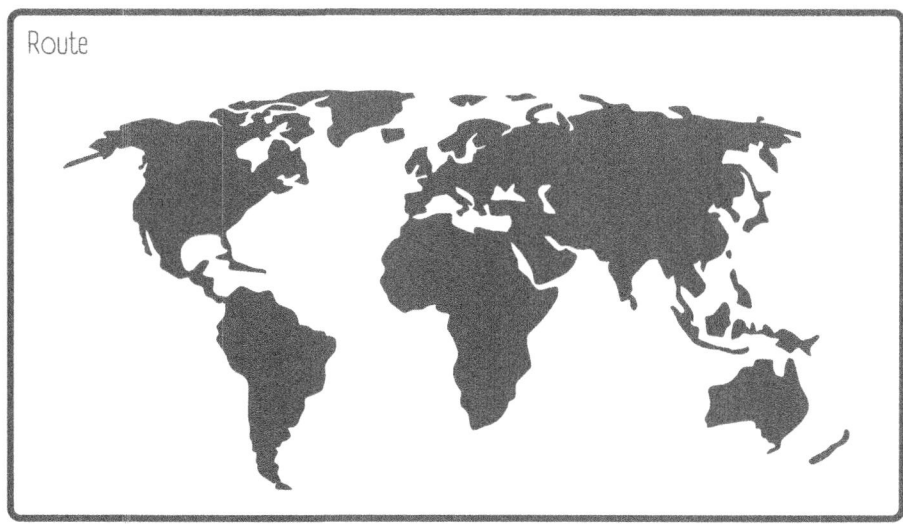

Date: ....

Departure Location	Departure Time
Stopover	Time
Arrival Location	Date & Time

Weather	
Wind	
Forecast	
Visibility	
Wave	

Course / Coordinates	
Speed	
Distance	
Crew	

Sketch	Notes

Photo

Anecdotes / Special Moments

Route

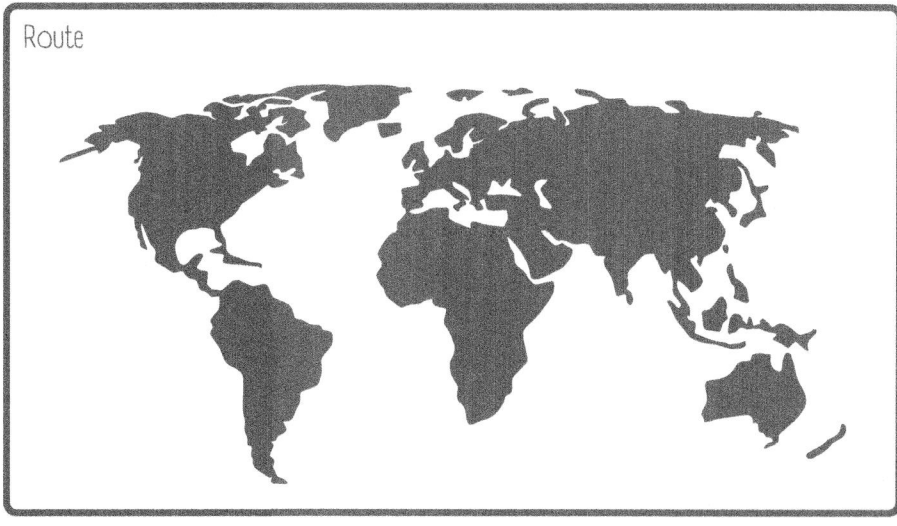

Date: _____

Departure Location	Departure Time
Stopover	Time
Arrival Location	Date & Time

Weather
Wind
Forecast
Visibility
Wave

Course / Coordinates
Speed
Distance
Crew

Sketch	Notes

Photo

Anecdotes / Special Moments

Route

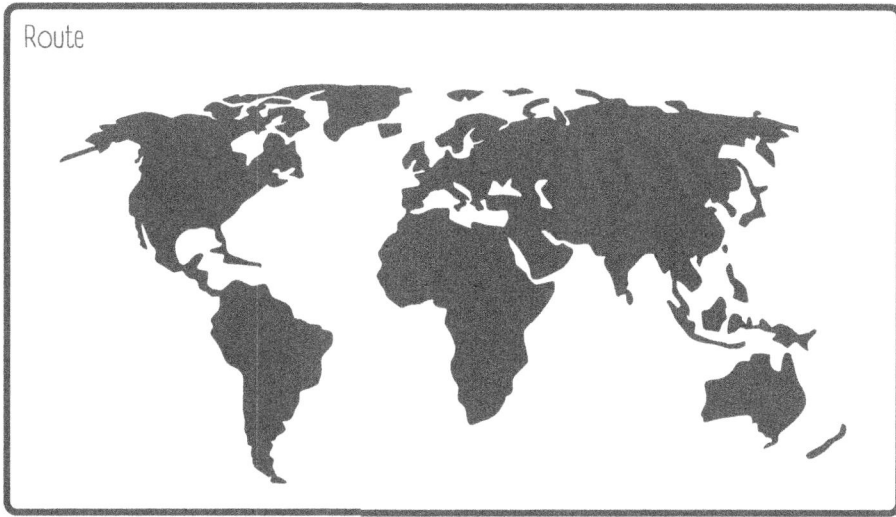

Date: ....

Departure Location	Departure Time
Stopover	Time
Arrival Location	Date & Time

Weather
Wind
Forecast
Visibility
Wave

Course / Coordinates
Speed
Distance
Crew

Sketch	Notes

Photo

Anecdotes / Special Moments

Route

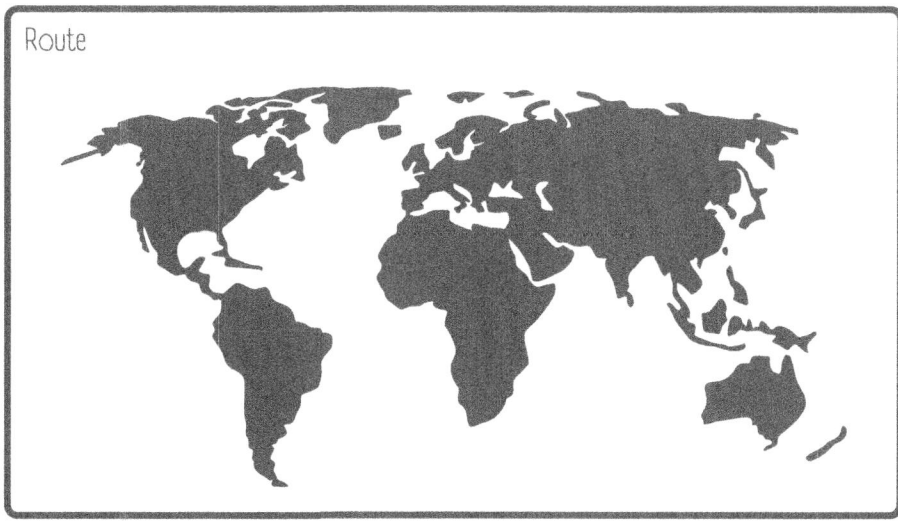

Date: _____

Departure Location	Departure Time
Stopover	Time
Arrival Location	Date & Time

Weather
Wind
Forecast
Visibility
Wave

Course / Coordinates
Speed
Distance
Crew

Sketch	Notes

Photo

Anecdotes / Special Moments

Route

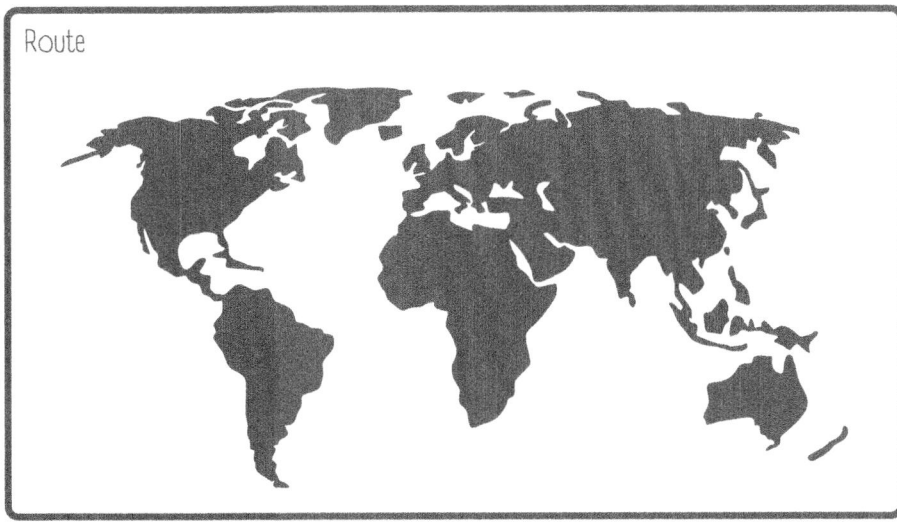

Date: ....

Departure Location	Departure Time
Stopover	Time
Arrival Location	Date & Time

Weather
Wind
Forecast
Visibility
Wave

Course / Coordinates
Speed
Distance
Crew

Sketch	Notes

Photo

Anecdotes / Special Moments

Route

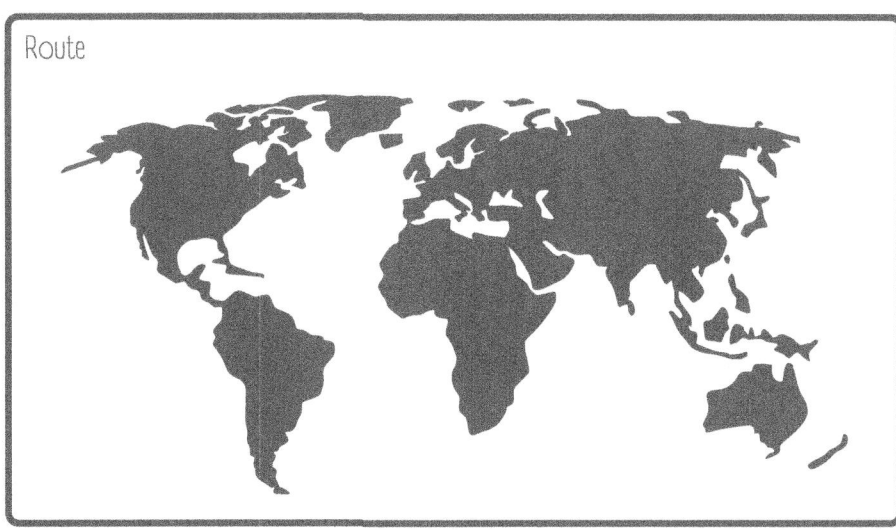

Date: _____

Departure Location	Departure Time
Stopover	Time
Arrival Location	Date & Time

Weather
Wind
Forecast
Visibility
Wave

Course / Coordinates
Speed
Distance
Crew

Sketch	Notes

Photo

Anecdotes / Special Moments

Route

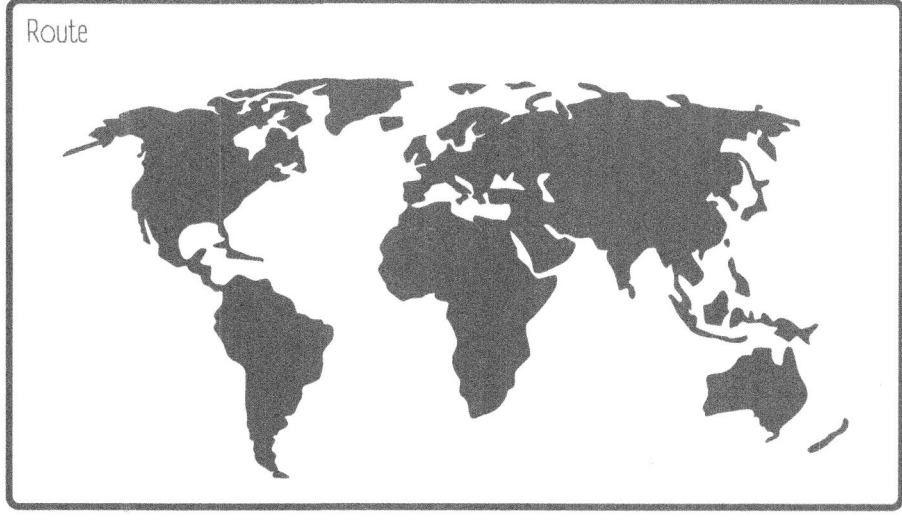

Date: _____

Departure Location	Departure Time
Stopover	Time
Arrival Location	Date & Time

Weather
Wind
Forecast
Visibility
Wave

Course / Coordinates
Speed
Distance
Crew

Sketch	Notes

Photo

Anecdotes / Special Moments

Route
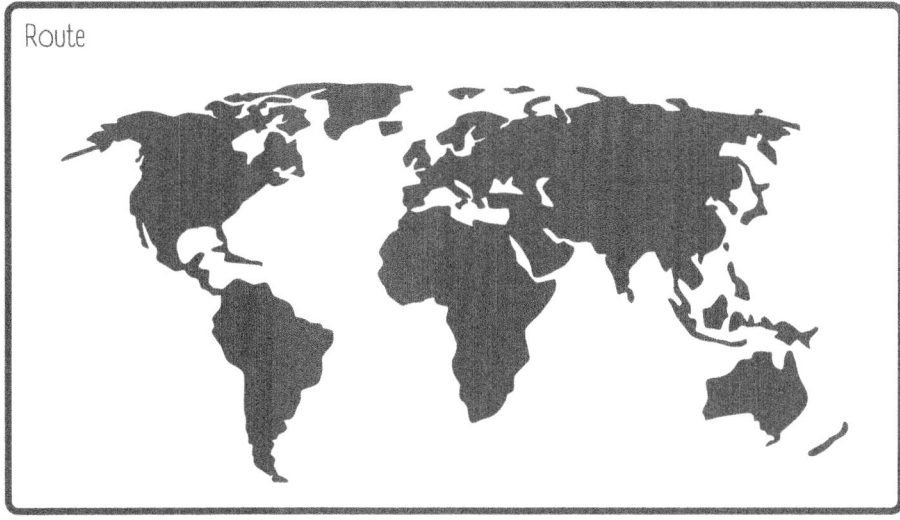

Date: _____

Departure Location	Departure Time
Stopover	Time
Arrival Location	Date & Time

Weather	
Wind	
Forecast	
Visibility	
Wave	

Course / Coordinates	
Speed	
Distance	
Crew	

Sketch	Notes

Photo

Anecdotes / Special Moments

Route

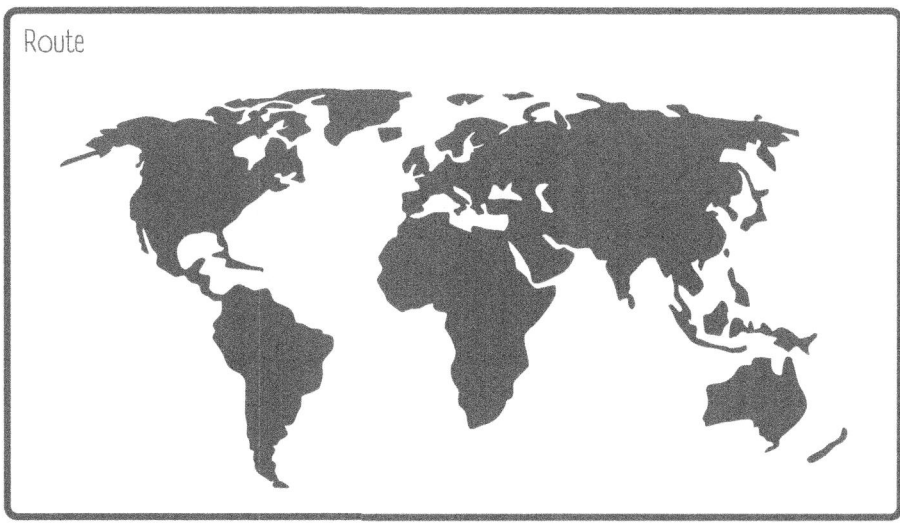

Date: ....

Departure Location	Departure Time
Stopover	Time
Arrival Location	Date & Time

Weather
Wind
Forecast
Visibility
Wave

Course / Coordinates
Speed
Distance
Crew

Sketch	Notes

Photo

Anecdotes / Special Moments

Route

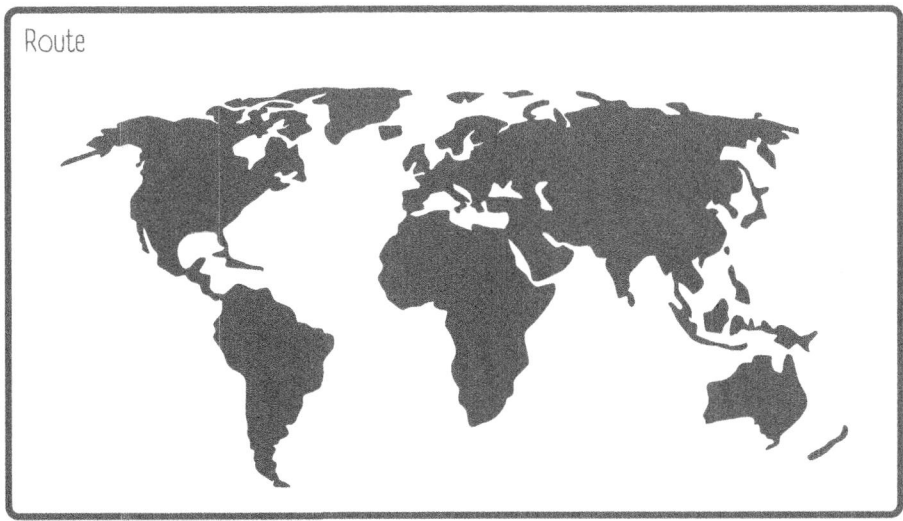

Date: ....

Departure Location	Departure Time
Stopover	Time
Arrival Location	Date & Time

Weather
Wind
Forecast
Visibility
Wave

Course / Coordinates
Speed
Distance
Crew

Sketch	Notes

Photo

Anecdotes / Special Moments

Route

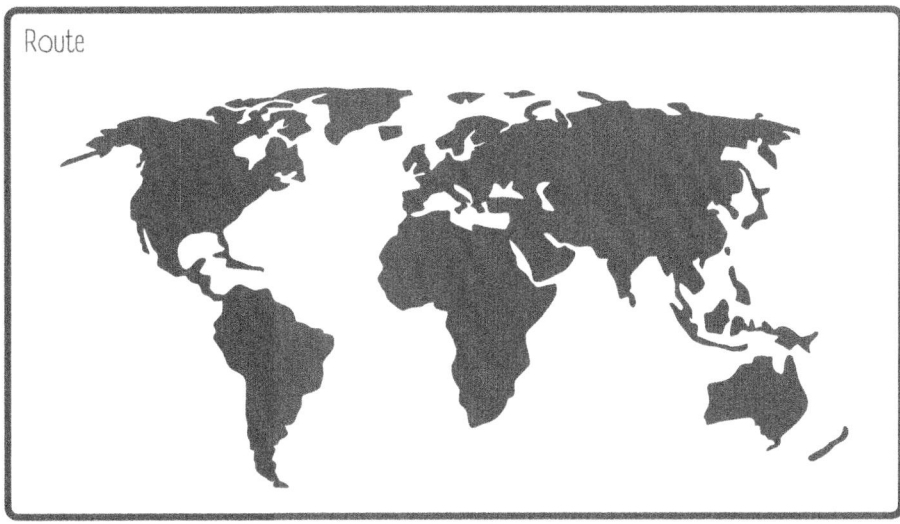

Date: _____

Departure Location	Departure Time
Stopover	Time
Arrival Location	Date & Time

Weather
Wind
Forecast
Visibility
Wave

Course / Coordinates
Speed
Distance
Crew

Sketch	Notes

Photo

Anecdotes / Special Moments

Route

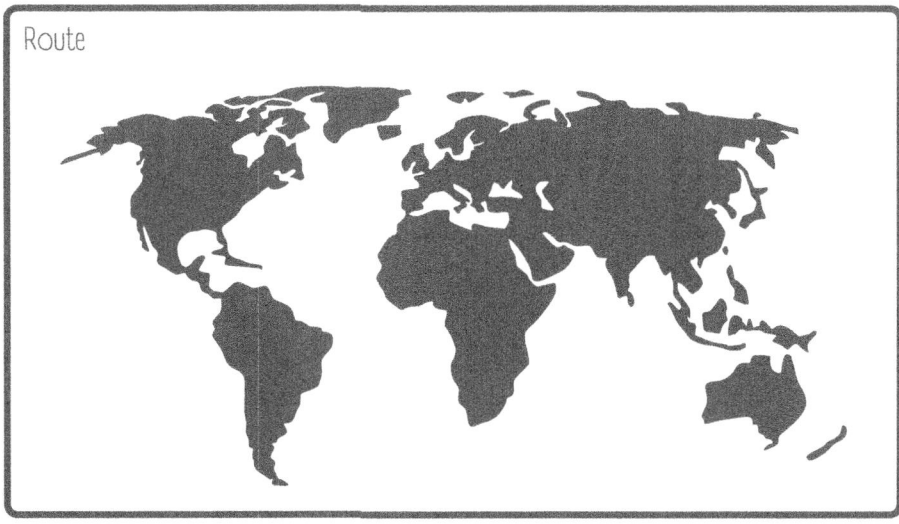

Date: _____

Departure Location	Departure Time
Stopover	Time
Arrival Location	Date & Time

Weather
Wind
Forecast
Visibility
Wave

Course / Coordinates
Speed
Distance
Crew

Sketch	Notes

Photo

Anecdotes / Special Moments

Route

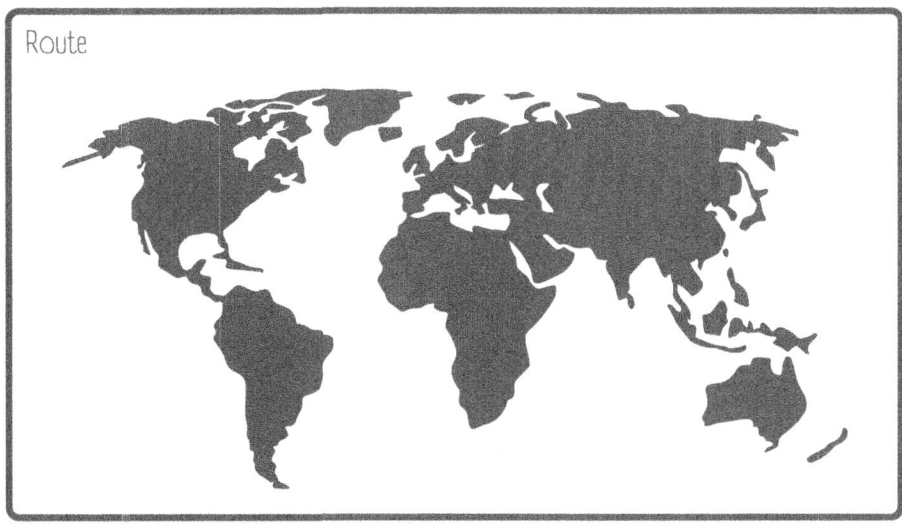

Date: _____

Departure Location	Departure Time
Stopover	Time
Arrival Location	Date & Time

Weather
Wind
Forecast
Visibility
Wave

Course / Coordinates
Speed
Distance
Crew

Sketch	Notes

Photo

Anecdotes / Special Moments

Route

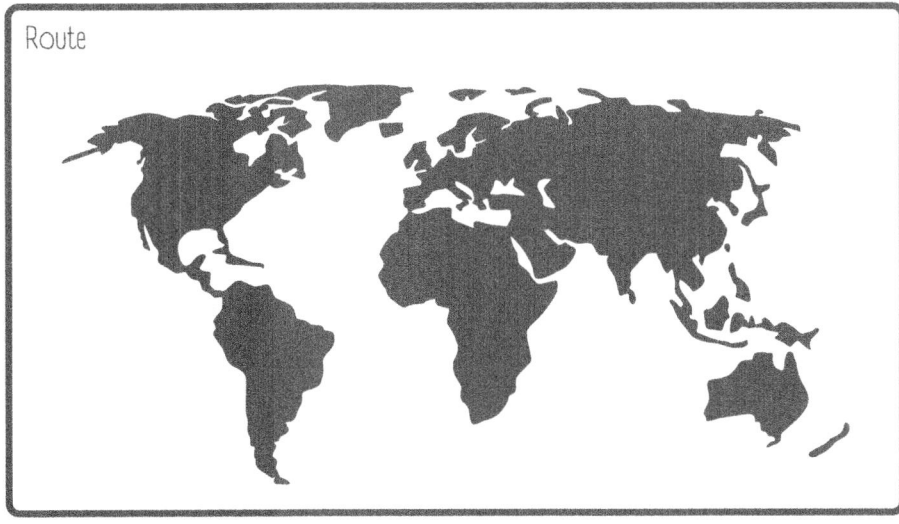

Date: ....

Departure Location	Departure Time
Stopover	Time
Arrival Location	Date & Time

Weather
Wind
Forecast
Visibility
Wave

Course / Coordinates
Speed
Distance
Crew

Sketch	Notes

Photo

Anecdotes / Special Moments

Route

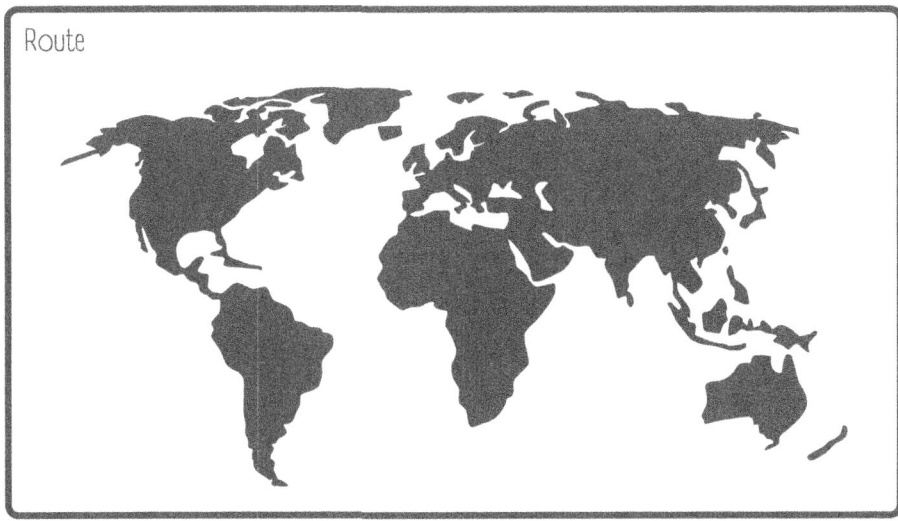

Date: ....

Departure Location	Departure Time
Stopover	Time
Arrival Location	Date & Time

Weather
Wind
Forecast
Visibility
Wave

Course / Coordinates
Speed
Distance
Crew

Sketch	Notes

Photo

Anecdotes / Special Moments

Route

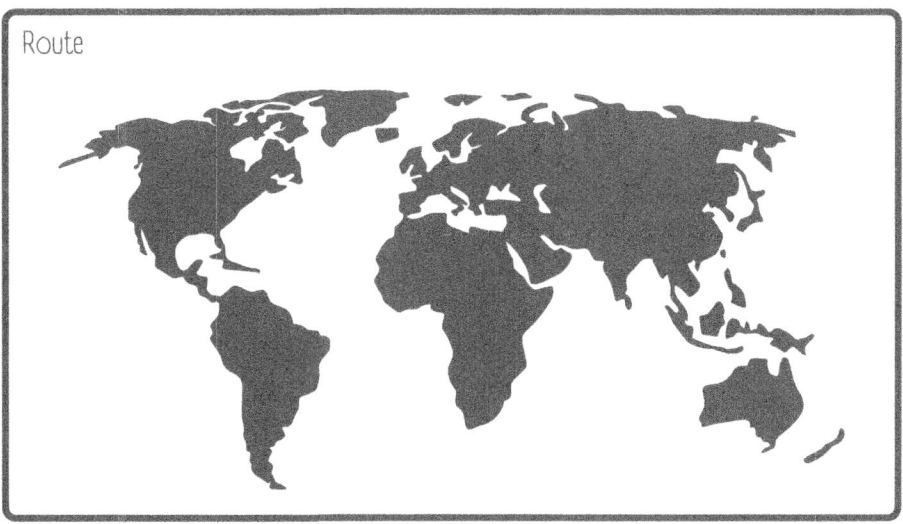

Date: ....

Departure Location	Departure Time
Stopover	Time
Arrival Location	Date & Time

Weather
Wind
Forecast
Visibility
Wave

Course / Coordinates
Speed
Distance
Crew

Sketch	Notes

Photo

Anecdotes / Special Moments

Route

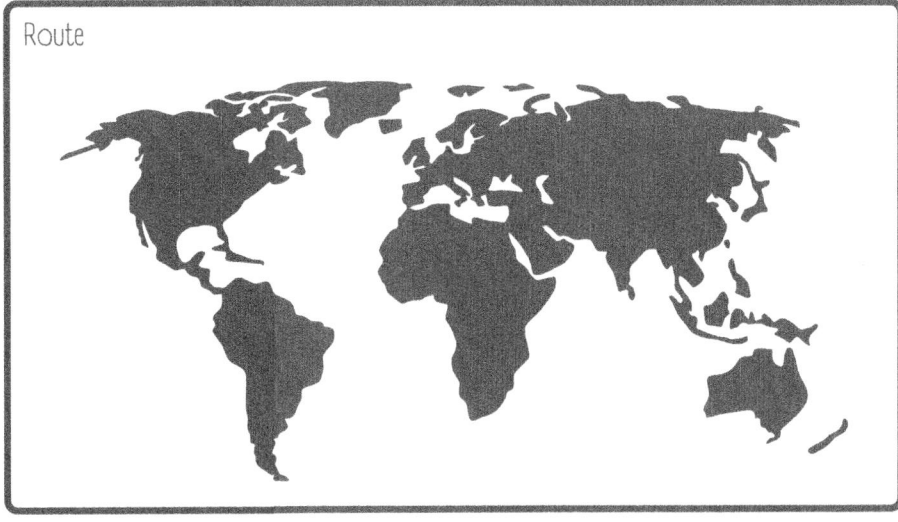

Date:

Departure Location	Departure Time
Stopover	Time
Arrival Location	Date & Time

Weather
Wind
Forecast
Visibility
Wave

Course / Coordinates
Speed
Distance
Crew

Sketch	Notes

Photo

Anecdotes / Special Moments

Route

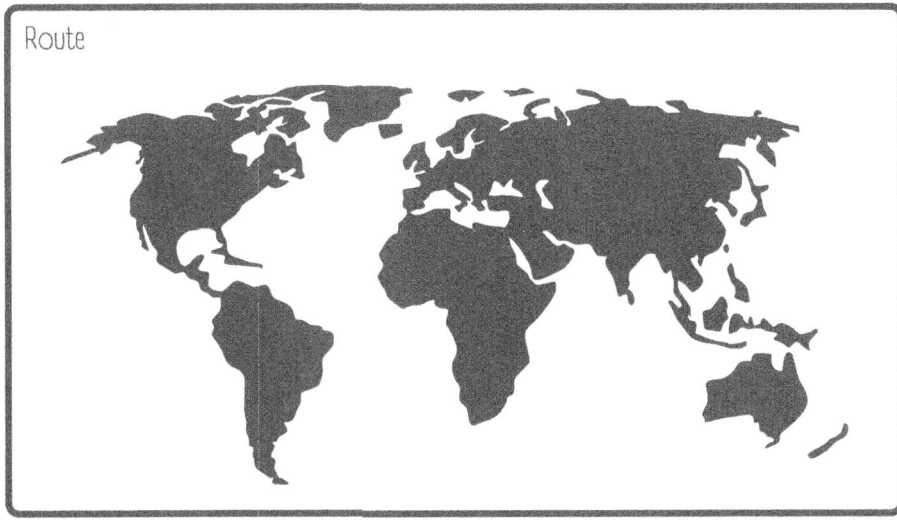

Date:

Departure Location	Departure Time
Stopover	Time
Arrival Location	Date & Time

Weather
Wind
Forecast
Visibility
Wave

Course / Coordinates
Speed
Distance
Crew

Sketch	Notes

Photo

Anecdotes / Special Moments

Route

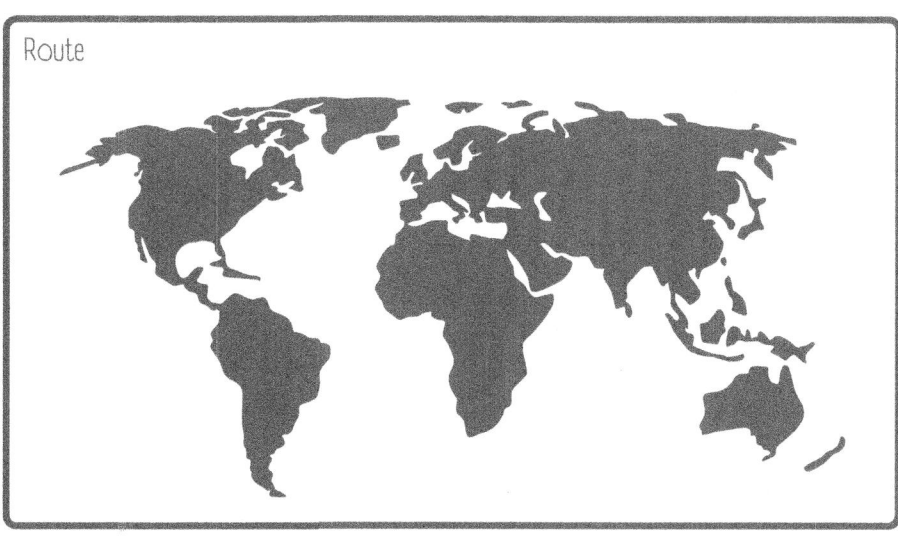

Date: _____

Departure Location	Departure Time
Stopover	Time
Arrival Location	Date & Time

Weather
Wind
Forecast
Visibility
Wave

Course / Coordinates
Speed
Distance
Crew

Sketch	Notes

Photo

Anecdotes / Special Moments

Route

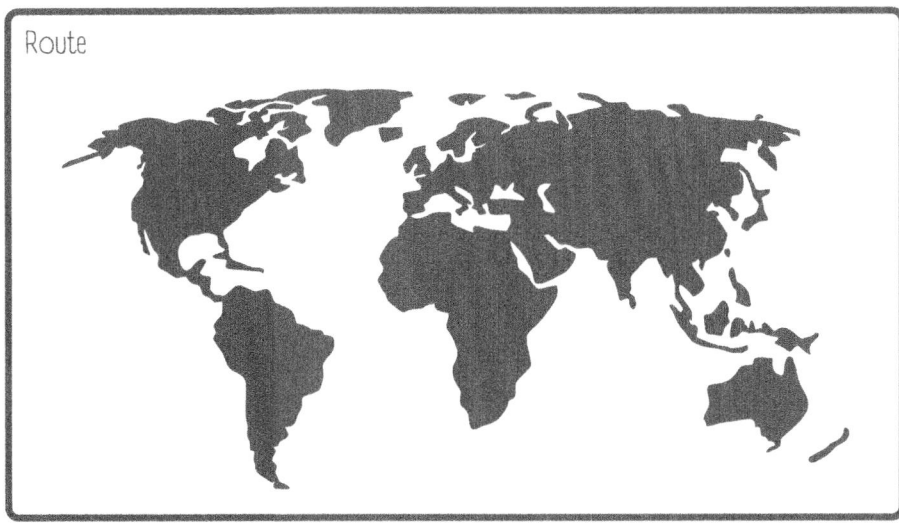

Date:

Departure Location	Departure Time
Stopover	Time
Arrival Location	Date & Time

Weather	
Wind	
Forecast	
Visibility	
Wave	

Course / Coordinates	
Speed	
Distance	
Crew	

Sketch	Notes

Photo

Anecdotes / Special Moments

Route

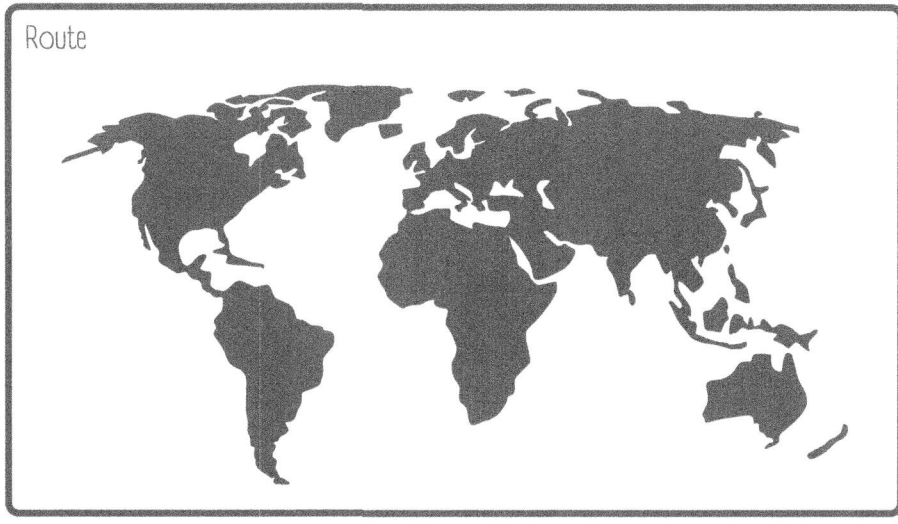

Date: ....

Departure Location	Departure Time
Stopover	Time
Arrival Location	Date & Time

Weather
Wind
Forecast
Visibility
Wave

Course / Coordinates
Speed
Distance
Crew

Sketch	Notes

Photo

Anecdotes / Special Moments

Route

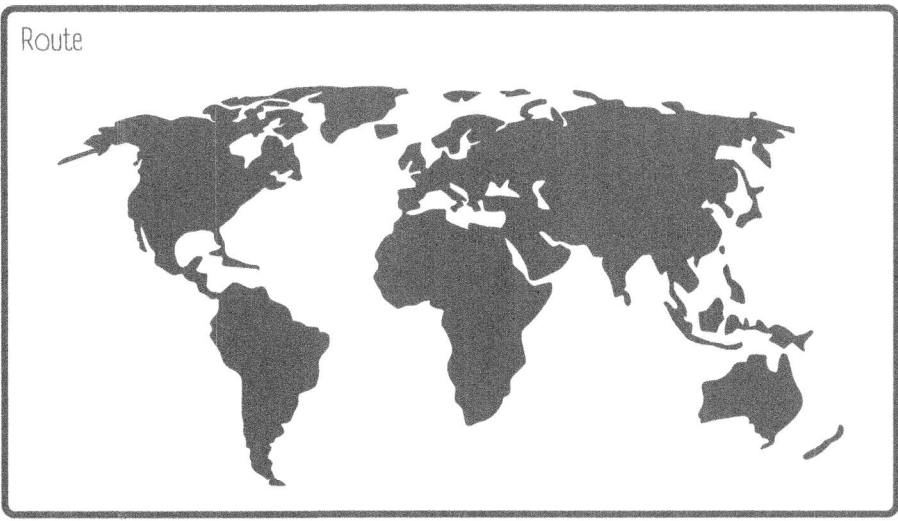

Date: _____

Departure Location	Departure Time
Stopover	Time
Arrival Location	Date & Time

- Weather
- Wind
- Forecast
- Visibility
- Wave

- Course / Coordinates
- Speed
- Distance
- Crew

Sketch

Notes

Photo

Anecdotes / Special Moments

Route

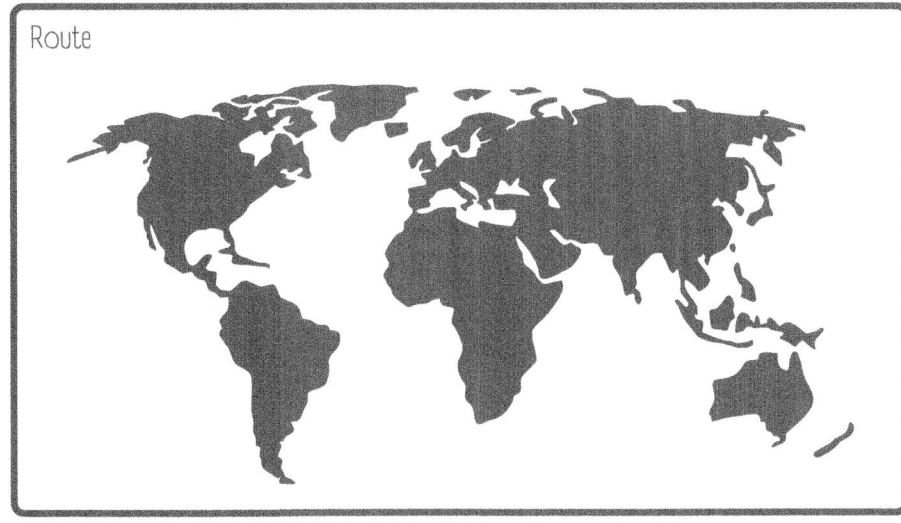

Date: ....

Departure Location	Departure Time
Stopover	Time
Arrival Location	Date & Time

Weather
Wind
Forecast
Visibility
Wave

Course / Coordinates
Speed
Distance
Crew

Sketch	Notes

Photo

Anecdotes / Special Moments

Route

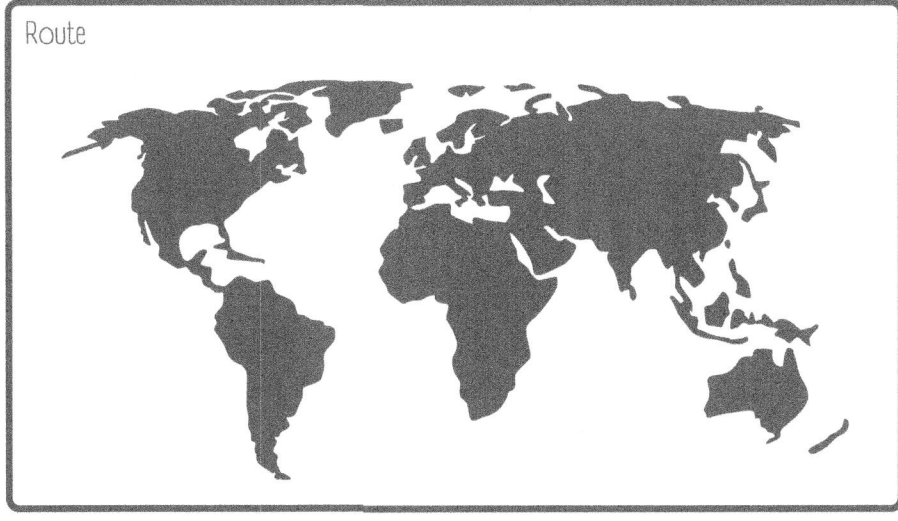

Date:

Departure Location	Departure Time
Stopover	Time
Arrival Location	Date & Time

Weather	
Wind	
Forecast	
Visibility	
Wave	

Course / Coordinates	
Speed	
Distance	
Crew	

Sketch	Notes

Photo

Anecdotes / Special Moments

Route

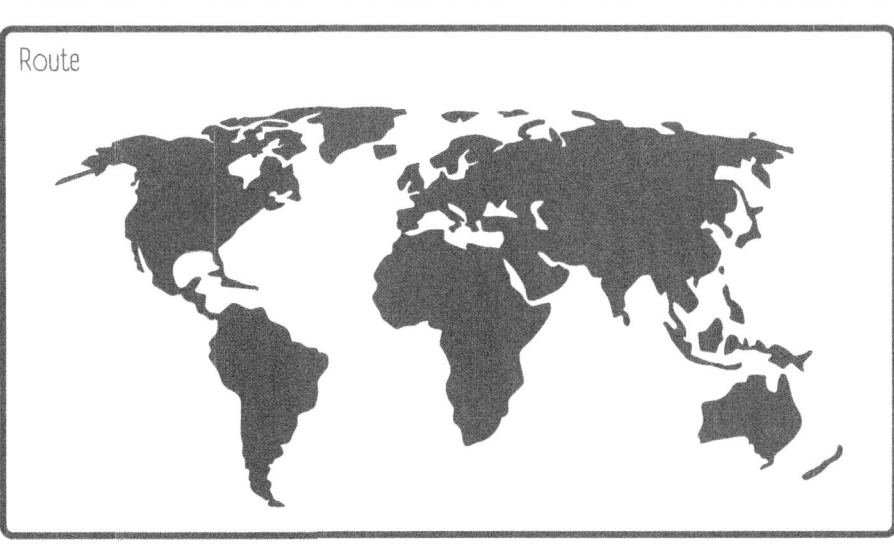

Date: ....

Departure Location	Departure Time
Stopover	Time
Arrival Location	Date & Time

Weather
Wind
Forecast
Visibility
Wave

Course / Coordinates
Speed
Distance
Crew

Sketch	Notes

Photo

Anecdotes / Special Moments

Route

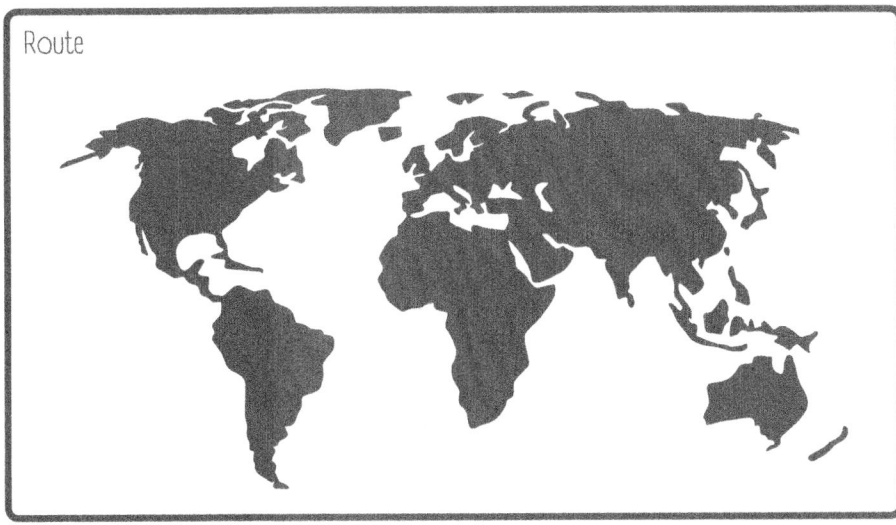

Date: ....

Departure Location	Departure Time
Stopover	Time
Arrival Location	Date & Time

Weather
Wind
Forecast
Visibility
Wave

Course / Coordinates
Speed
Distance
Crew

Sketch	Notes

Photo

Anecdotes / Special Moments

Route

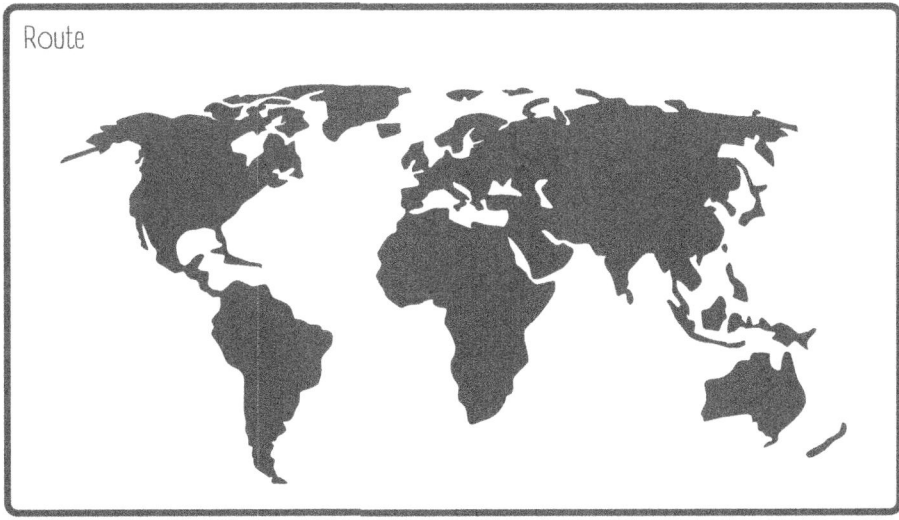

Date: ....

Departure Location	Departure Time
Stopover	Time
Arrival Location	Date & Time

Weather	
Wind	
Forecast	
Visibility	
Wave	

Course / Coordinates	
Speed	
Distance	
Crew	

Sketch	Notes

Photo

Anecdotes / Special Moments

Route

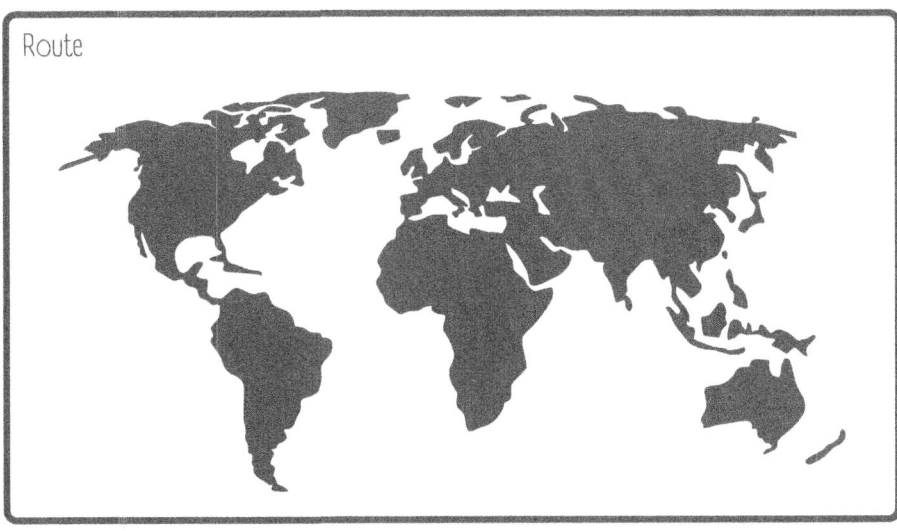

Date: _____

Departure Location	Departure Time
Stopover	Time
Arrival Location	Date & Time

Weather
Wind
Forecast
Visibility
Wave

Course / Coordinates
Speed
Distance
Crew

Sketch	Notes

Photo

Anecdotes / Special Moments

Route

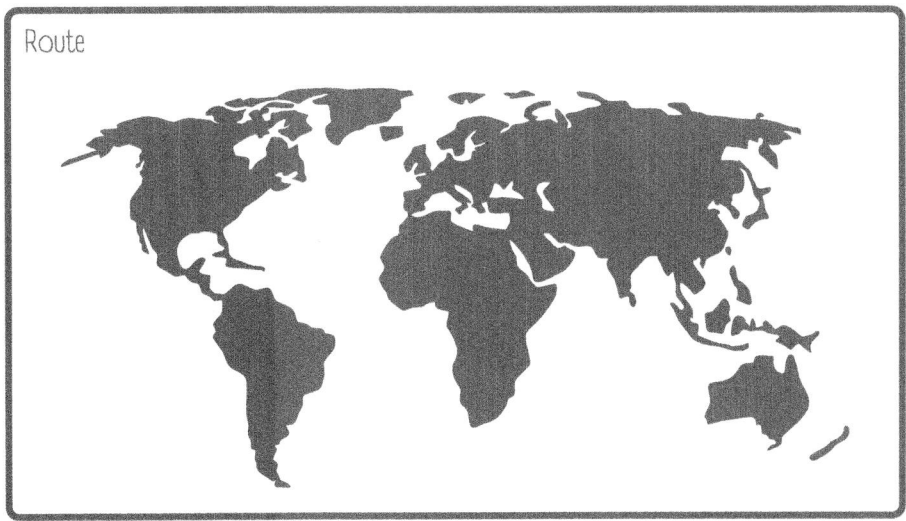

Date: ....

Departure Location	Departure Time
Stopover	Time
Arrival Location	Date & Time

Weather
Wind
Forecast
Visibility
Wave

Course / Coordinates
Speed
Distance
Crew

Sketch	Notes

Photo

Anecdotes / Special Moments

Route

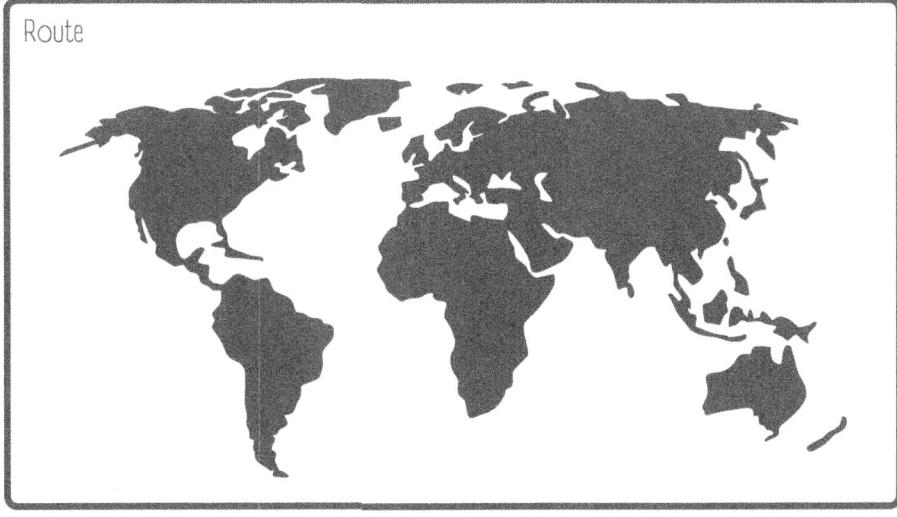

Copyright Julia Seyfarth,
Nessetal 2021
Alle Rechte vorbehalten
Text und Buchgestaltung:
Julia Seyfarth
julia.seyfarth2020@gmail.com

Printed in Great Britain
by Amazon